Curious Kids Guides
REPTILES

Amanda O'Neill

KINGFISHER

NEW YORK

REPTILES

KINGFISHER
Larousse Kingfisher Chambers Inc.
80 Maiden Lane
New York, New York 10038
www.kingfisherpub.com

First published in 1994
First published in this format 2002
10 9 8 7 6 5 4 3 2 1
1TR/1201/TIMS/*UD UNV/128MA

LIBRARY OF CONGRESS CATALOGING-IN-PUBLICATION DATA
has been applied for.

ISBN 0-7534-5467-X

Printed in China

Series editor: Clare Oliver
Series designer: David West Children's Books
Author: Amanda O'Neill
Consultant: Michael Chinery
Editor: Claire Llewelyn, Art editor: Christina Fraser
Picture researcher: Amanda Francis
Illustrations: Peter Dennis (Linda Rogers Associates) 6-7, 24bl, 25tr; Chris Forsey 10-11, 30-31; Craig Greenwood (Wildlife Art Agency) 14-15, 26-27; Stephen Holmes 16bl; Tony Kenyon (BL Kearley) all cartoons; Alan Male (Linden Artists) 12-13; Nicki Palin 16-17, 28-29; Luis Rey 24-25; Andrea Ricciardi di Gaudesi 20-21; David Wright (Kathy Jakeman) cover, 4-5, 8-9, 18-19, 22-23.

CONTENTS

Which animals are reptiles?

Snakes, lizards, crocodiles, and turtles all belong to the same animal group—the reptiles. All reptiles have a bony skeleton and a scaly skin. Most of them lay eggs, which hatch on land. But some reptiles give birth to their babies.

Lizard

● Reptiles live on land and in the sea almost everywhere on Earth. But they don't like the cold, so you won't find them around the Poles.

Crocodile

Are frogs and newts reptiles?

Frogs and newts are not reptiles. They have no scales, and their skin is very thin. They lay their eggs in water, and their young hatch out as tadpoles. Baby reptiles look just like their parents, only smaller.

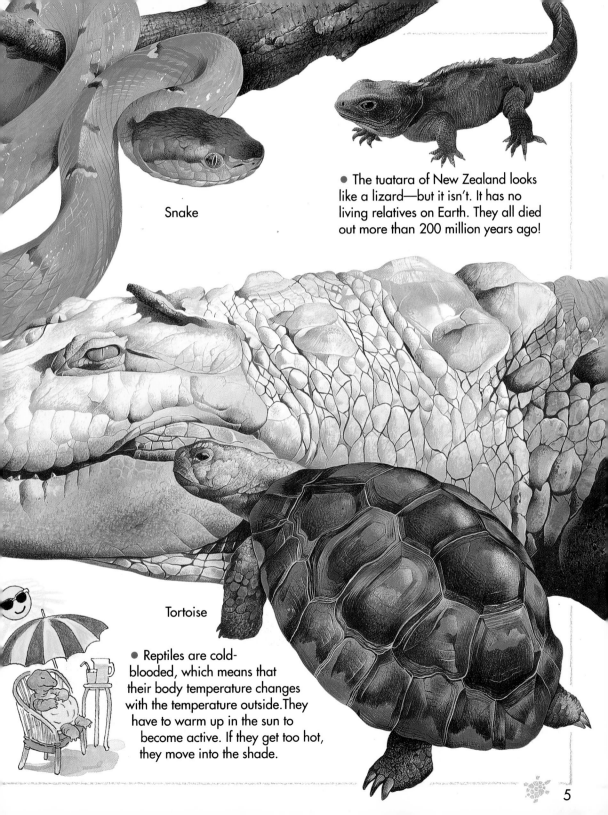

Snake

● The tuatara of New Zealand looks like a lizard—but it isn't. It has no living relatives on Earth. They all died out more than 200 million years ago!

Tortoise

● Reptiles are cold-blooded, which means that their body temperature changes with the temperature outside. They have to warm up in the sun to become active. If they get too hot, they move into the shade.

Which is the biggest reptile?

The world's biggest reptile is the saltwater crocodile of tropical Asia and Australia. This huge beast can grow to about 23 feet—as wide as a soccer goal.

● The fastest reptile is a North American lizard called the six-lined racerunner. It could easily outrun you in a race—over short distances it reaches speeds of 18 miles an hour!

Which reptile lives the longest?

Tortoises can live to a ripe old age. The oldest one ever known lived to be 152 years old! But this might not be a record—there could be even older tortoises in the wild.

• The smallest reptile is a tiny gecko lizard from the West Indies. It measures 1.5 inches from nose to tail and would fit inside a book of matches with room to spare.

Which is the biggest snake?

The biggest snake is the anaconda of South America, which grows up to 33 feet—that's as long as a bus. The reticulated python is another whopper, but although it's as long as the anaconda, it's not as heavy.

Do snakes have good table manners?

Snakes are not polite at mealtimes. They don't chew a meal, they swallow it whole! They stretch their mouths over their food, until it's all gone. And their jaws and body are so elastic that they can eat things much fatter than themselves.

● Most snakes are loners, but hundreds of rattlesnakes will snuggle together underground to sleep through the cold winter months.

● Snakes can bend and twist because their backbones are made up of hundreds of tiny bones, all linked together like a chain.

Why do snakes have teeth and fangs?

As well as having teeth to grip its food, a poisonous snake also has a pair of fangs. It uses these long teeth to strike its prey and inject it with poison, which shoots out of holes at the tips of the fangs.

● Vipers have extra-long fangs that fold down flat when they're not in use. It's just as well—the vipers wouldn't be able to shut their mouths otherwise!

Why do snakes stare?

Snakes stare because they can't blink. And they can't blink because they have no eyelids. Each eye is covered with a see-through scale that protects the eye. Snakes get brand-new scales every time they shed their skins.

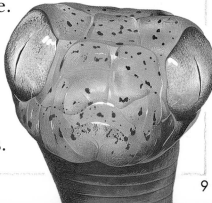

Whose tongue is longer than its tail?

The chameleon's sticky-tipped tongue isn't just longer than its tail, it's longer than its whole body! The lizard shoots it out quick as a wink and reels it back in with a meal.

Why do lizards lose their tails?

Lizards can snap off their tails when they're being attacked. The dropped tail wriggles, puzzling the enemy, and giving the lizard time to escape. A new tail grows in a few weeks.

Why do geckos lick their eyes?

Most lizards have eyelids to wipe their eyes, but the gecko doesn't. Like a snake, it has a scale across the eye. To keep its eyes moist and squeaky clean, the gecko licks them, using its long tongue like a washcloth.

● Most lizards are land-lubbers. The marine iguana from the Galápagos Islands is the only one that swims in the ocean.

Are there still dragons on Earth?

The Komodo dragon may not have wings or breathe fire, but it is truly awesome. It's the world's largest lizard—longer than a car, and heavier than a couple of prizefighters. When people first saw one about 100 years ago, they thought they were looking at a dragon!

Which reptile is a living fortress?

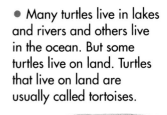

● Many turtles live in lakes and rivers and others live in the ocean. But some turtles live on land. Turtles that live on land are usually called tortoises.

Living inside a shell is like living inside a fortress. At the first sign of danger, a tortoise retreats inside the shell's thick walls, blocking the "doors" with its feet and claws. It's well protected from attack, and from heat and cold too.

● A tortoise could never park its shell and leave it behind. The shell's horny plates are joined to the skeleton underneath.

Do turtles have teeth?

Turtles don't have teeth, but their horny beaks have plenty of bite. Alligator snapping turtles are particularly fierce. One bite from them and you could lose your toes!

● A tortoise's damaged shell will slowly heal. A vet can help by patching it with fiberglass, a light material used to build boats.

Which turtle breathes through a snorkel?

The spiny soft-shelled turtle spends most of its time under water in rivers and ponds. It doesn't need to come up to the surface to breathe. It pokes its long snout out of the water like a snorkel and draws in a noseful of air.

● Turtles were swimming in the ocean more than 200 million years ago. They're the most ancient of all reptiles.

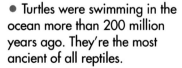

● A tortoise's shell keeps out most enemies, but eagles and vultures have cracked the problem. They drop the poor animals from a great height and smash their shells.

Which animal is like a submarine?

An alligator lies so low in the water that it's hidden like a submarine. Its eyes, ears, and nostrils all lie on the top of its head, so that it can still see, hear, and smell things while most of its body is under the water. Other animals don't even know it's there—until it grabs them!

● Crocodiles are fully waterproof! When they dive, special flaps seal off their ears, throat, and nostrils, and extra eyelids act like underwater goggles.

Alligator

● It's easy to tell an alligator from a crocodile. If all the bottom teeth are tucked inside the mouth, it's an alligator. If the fourth bottom tooth sticks out, it's a croc.

Gavial

● Gavials belong to the same group as crocodiles and alligators.

What makes a crocodile smile?

A crocodile never smiles, but it looks as though it does. It is actually panting to let its body heat escape through its mouth, cooling the animal down.

Crocodile

● Did you know that crocodiles go to the dentist? They open their mouths and let plovers hop inside. The birds pull out bits of old food and any little insects that they find there.

Why do crocodiles eat together?

When one crocodile makes a kill, as many as 40 friends will join in the meal. It might look like a tug-of-war, but the animals help each other by tearing off chunks that are small enough to swallow.

● Did you know that crocodiles eat stones? The weight keeps them low in the water, so they can hide from their prey.

How do lizards move in a hurry?

Some lizards find they can move much more quickly if they run on just two legs instead of on all fours. When something disturbs a crested water dragon and frightens it, it likes to make a speedy getaway. So the lizard stands up, pushes on its powerful back legs and hurries off just as fast as its legs will take it.

How do snakes move without legs?

Snakes manage very well without legs. One of the ways they move is by forming their bodies into zigzags. By pushing against the surface, they force themselves forward. Many snakes are good swimmers and tree-climbers, some burrow underground, and others even glide through the air.

• Geckos can walk upside down, thanks to tiny hairs on their feet. They have up to 150,000 hooked hairs on each toe. These stick like Velcro to whatever they touch—even a slippery pane of glass!

• Tortoises are never in a hurry. Most of them would take three hours or more to cross a football field.

How do crocodiles swim without fins?

Crocodiles may not have fins like a fish, but they have very powerful tails. By lashing them from side to side, the crocodiles use their tails to propel them through the water. The animals tuck their legs very close to their bodies to make themselves as smooth and as streamlined as possible. That way they slip along easily— and incredibly fast.

Which lizard looks both ways at once?

A chameleon's eyes swivel like gun turrets and can even move in different directions. This doubles the lizard's chances of spotting something to eat and makes it very difficult for a moth to sneak by without being seen!

Why does a snake flick its tongue?

As a snake's tongue darts in and out, it picks up scents in the air. The tongue carries these up to a sensitive area in the roof of the mouth, which tastes the air. It sends messages to the brain, telling it whether a mate, a meal, or an enemy is near.

● Alligators are the noisiest reptiles. They don't just "talk" to each other, they bellow! In the mating season, males make a great uproar as they try to attract females.

● When the cave anole lizard comes out into the sunshine, it closes its eyes and peers through scales in its lower eyelids. These protect its eyes like a pair of sunglasses!

What use is a hole in the head?

If you're a lizard, a hole in the head is very useful—because it's probably an ear! Most lizards have an ear on each side of the head. It's just an open hole leading down to the eardrum inside. Reptiles' ears don't stick out from their heads as ours do. And snakes' ears are hidden inside their heads.

● Rattlesnakes and other pit vipers can hunt in total darkness. They can sense the body heat of a nearby animal and strike their prey with amazing accuracy.

19

Why do some reptiles disguise themselves?

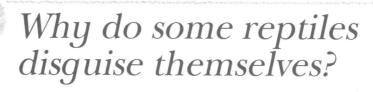

Reptiles use disguises to hide themselves away. Some of them hide to help them get a good meal. A hidden hunter blends in with the background and won't be seen until it pounces on its prey. Other reptiles hide to protect themselves. They don't want to become someone else's lunch! And some reptiles have markings that make them look more dangerous than they really are.

● The milk snake is completely harmless, but it protects itself from enemies by pretending to be dangerous. It wears the same color stripes as the poisonous coral snake. Can you spot the difference?

Coral snake

Milk snake

● Chameleons are the masters of disguise. They can change their color to match their surroundings —well, almost!

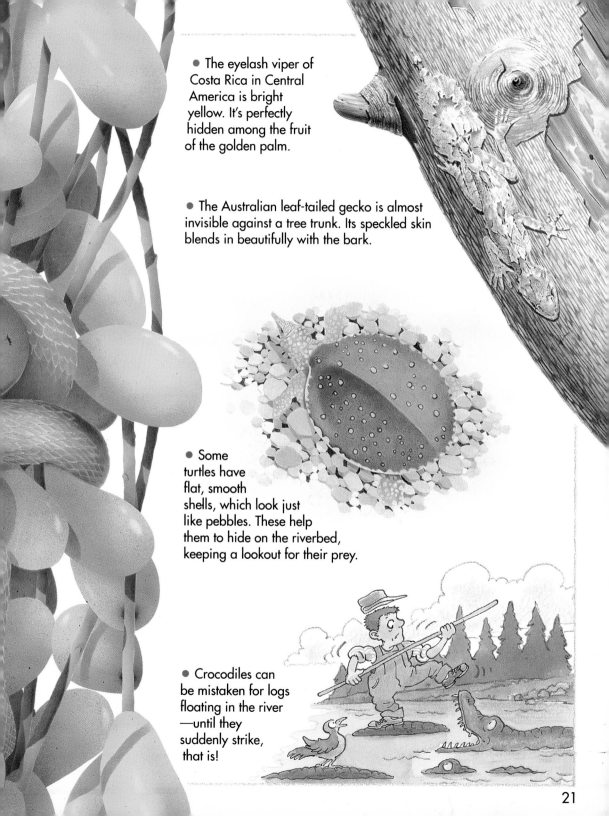

- The eyelash viper of Costa Rica in Central America is bright yellow. It's perfectly hidden among the fruit of the golden palm.

- The Australian leaf-tailed gecko is almost invisible against a tree trunk. Its speckled skin blends in beautifully with the bark.

- Some turtles have flat, smooth shells, which look just like pebbles. These help them to hide on the riverbed, keeping a lookout for their prey.

- Crocodiles can be mistaken for logs floating in the river —until they suddenly strike, that is!

Which lizard has a frightful frill?

If you frighten an Australian frilled lizard, it will try to frighten you back. It has a frill of skin around its neck, which it can open up like an umbrella. This makes the lizard look twice its real size. And when it stretches its mouth wide open too, it's a pretty terrifying sight!

- Steer clear of the horned toad from the Southwest. It isn't really a toad, it's a lizard, and it can squirt jets of blood—from its eyes! Scary!

- The African pancake tortoise is well named. It's flat enough to wriggle down a crack in a rock. But then it cleverly puffs itself up, so no enemy can tug it out!

Which turtle kicks up a stink?

The stinkpot turtle has earned its name! When it feels threatened, it lets out a yucky smell that quickly drives away its enemies. And they don't come back!

Why do some snakes pretend to be dead?

• The stumpy-tailed skink has a stumpy tail the same shape as its head. As long as it keeps its mouth shut, its enemies can't tell whether the lizard is coming or going!

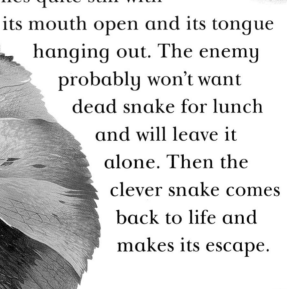

Some snakes face danger by pretending that they're dead. The European grass snake rolls on its back and lies quite still with its mouth open and its tongue hanging out. The enemy probably won't want dead snake for lunch and will leave it alone. Then the clever snake comes back to life and makes its escape.

Which turtle fishes with its tongue?

The alligator snapping turtle has a wriggly pink tip to its tongue that looks just like a worm. The turtle lies on the bottom of the lake with its mouth open. To any fish, the "worm" looks like dinner. But if the fish swims up hungrily, it's snapped up by the turtle instead!

● Most smaller lizards are meat eaters. They eat only insects or small animals. But the green anole makes sure it gets its vitamins and eats fruit as well!

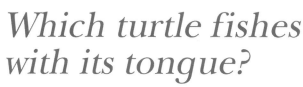

Who enjoys a mouthful of prickles?

Like many large lizards, the land iguana of the Galápagos Islands is a vegetarian. It likes nothing better than a cactus for supper and can munch on the spines without feeling any pain!

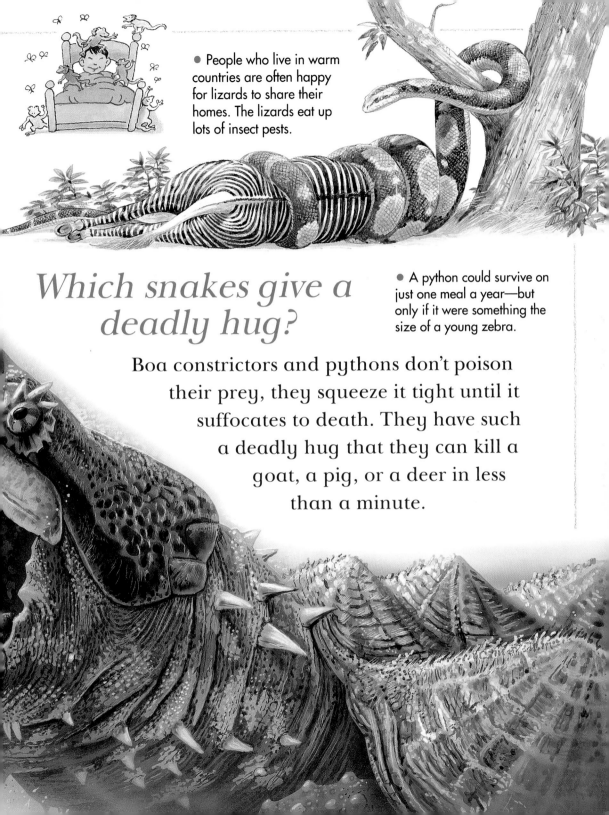

● People who live in warm countries are often happy for lizards to share their homes. The lizards eat up lots of insect pests.

Which snakes give a deadly hug?

● A python could survive on just one meal a year—but only if it were something the size of a young zebra.

Boa constrictors and pythons don't poison their prey, they squeeze it tight until it suffocates to death. They have such a deadly hug that they can kill a goat, a pig, or a deer in less than a minute.

Which reptile stays in its egg?

Young snakes take their time about hatching. Having broken open its shell, a youngster pokes out its head to look around. It may decide to stay safe inside for a day or two longer, before it slithers out to explore.

● Baby reptiles have a special tooth to cut their way out of the egg. It drops off once it's done its job.

Which reptile lays the most eggs?

A green turtle lays more than 1,000 eggs in a season in holes she has dug on the beach. Then she can be sure that at least some of her young will survive. Gulls, crabs, rats, foxes, and fish all feast on the tiny turtles. Only one turtle in 1,000 may grow to be an adult.

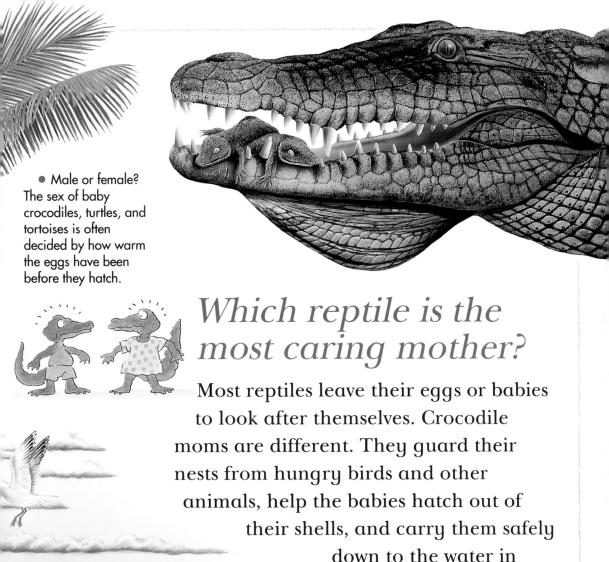

● Male or female? The sex of baby crocodiles, turtles, and tortoises is often decided by how warm the eggs have been before they hatch.

Which reptile is the most caring mother?

Most reptiles leave their eggs or babies to look after themselves. Crocodile moms are different. They guard their nests from hungry birds and other animals, help the babies hatch out of their shells, and carry them safely down to the water in their mouths.

Do reptiles have skin like ours?

A reptile's skin is quite tough and horny, more like our fingernails than our skin. On snakes and lizards, most of the skin is covered with small scales that overlap one another. But crocodiles and turtles have even tougher skins, with hard plates rather than scales.

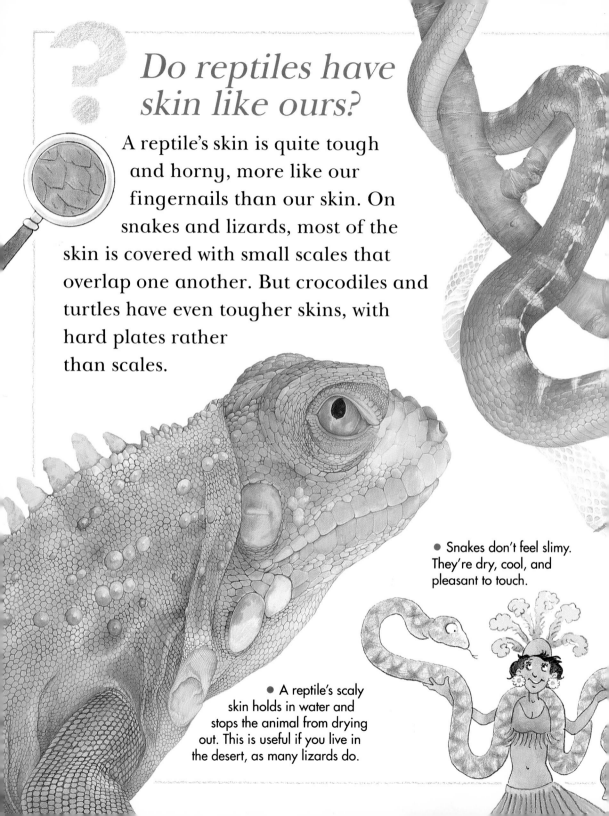

● Snakes don't feel slimy. They're dry, cool, and pleasant to touch.

● A reptile's scaly skin holds in water and stops the animal from drying out. This is useful if you live in the desert, as many lizards do.

● A snake's old skin begins to split at the lips. The snake wriggles out head first, turning the skin inside out as it goes. The skin often comes off in one piece, in a perfect snake shape.

Why do snakes shed their skins?

Like your old clothes, a snake's skin wears out and needs replacing—often in a bigger size. So from three to seven times a year, the old skin splits open and peels off, and— presto!—there's a brand-new skin waiting underneath.

● In times of danger, the armadillo lizard turns into an armored ball. It rolls on its back, grips its tail in its mouth and hides its soft belly behind a wall of scales and spines.

Why do some lizards have horns and spikes?

Horns and spikes are a good way of protecting an animal. Like a strong suit of armor, they make a lizard look fierce —and they also make a prickly mouthful for any animal that tries to attack.

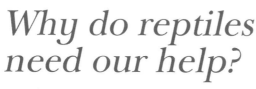

Why do reptiles need our help?

Many reptiles are in danger of dying out forever. In the past, some kinds of reptiles died out in the slow, natural process called evolution. But this takes thousands or millions of years. Today's reptiles are dying out much more quickly because people hunt them or destroy the places where they live.

● Many endangered reptiles are now being looked after in zoos. In time, their young may be returned to the wild.

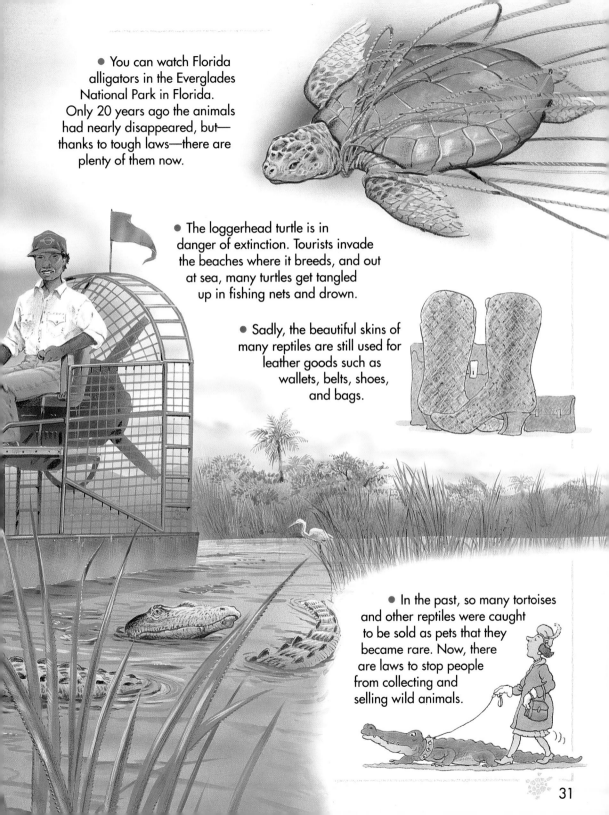

● You can watch Florida alligators in the Everglades National Park in Florida. Only 20 years ago the animals had nearly disappeared, but—thanks to tough laws—there are plenty of them now.

● The loggerhead turtle is in danger of extinction. Tourists invade the beaches where it breeds, and out at sea, many turtles get tangled up in fishing nets and drown.

● Sadly, the beautiful skins of many reptiles are still used for leather goods such as wallets, belts, shoes, and bags.

● In the past, so many tortoises and other reptiles were caught to be sold as pets that they became rare. Now, there are laws to stop people from collecting and selling wild animals.

Index